The RAG Revolution: Transforming AI Text Generation with Real-Time Data

A Step-by-Step Guide to Creating, Building Robust, and Scaling Retrieval-Augmented Generation Systems with Real-World Applications

Lena Fairford

TABLE OF CONTENT

Introduction to RAG and the Future of AI Text Generation

Retrieval-Augmented Generation (RAG) is revolutionizing the way AI systems generate text, combining the creative power of large language models (LLMs) with real-time, contextually relevant data. By leveraging the retrieval of information from vast databases, RAG enables more accurate, up-to-date, and grounded text generation, far surpassing the capabilities of traditional models. The importance of RAG lies in its ability to enhance the reliability of AI outputs, making them more contextually aware and reducing the occurrence of "hallucinations" or inaccurate results.

At the core of RAG lies the concept of augmenting the generative process by integrating external knowledge sources.

While traditional LLMs can generate text based only on the data they've been trained on, RAG systems access dynamic knowledge stores to provide fresh, accurate information that informs the model's generation process. This is particularly important in fields where precision and up-to-date knowledge are essential, such as healthcare, finance, and customer service. RAG helps bridge the gap between static model training and the rapidly evolving world of real-time data, enabling AI systems to generate text that is not just coherent but also grounded in verifiable facts.

The mechanics of RAG involve two main components: the **retrieval process** and the **generation process**. The retrieval process typically involves searching through vast knowledge databases, such as vector databases, to find relevant information based on a user's query.

Once relevant data is retrieved, the generative model integrates this information into the text it produces, ensuring the output is both creative and accurate. This hybrid approach of combining retrieval and generation enables AI systems to produce high-quality content, whether it's generating answers to specific questions, summarizing complex documents, or even creating personalized narratives.

One of the key technologies driving RAG is the **large language model (LLM)**, which acts as the generative engine in these systems. LLMs like GPT-3 and BERT have gained widespread attention for their ability to generate human-like text, but their limitations are also well-known. These models can only generate content based on the data they were trained on, and they have no ability to access or reference real-time information. RAG solves this problem by augmenting these models with access to dynamic data, enabling them to generate more accurate and relevant outputs.

Another critical technology in RAG systems is the **vector database**, which is used to store and retrieve knowledge efficiently. Unlike traditional relational databases, which store data in rows and columns, vector databases use high-dimensional vectors to represent data, making it easier for AI models to retrieve relevant information based on the similarity of the data points. This allows for fast and efficient retrieval of relevant content, which can then be integrated into the AI's text generation process. Tools like **Pinecone**, **Deep Lake**, and **FAISS** have become essential in RAG workflows, enabling scalable and efficient data retrieval.

The integration of RAG with LLMs and vector databases has led to significant advancements in **real-world applications**. In customer service, for example, chatbots powered by RAG can provide more accurate, real-time responses by pulling in relevant information from company databases, knowledge bases, or even the latest news articles.

In the healthcare industry, RAG systems can assist doctors by retrieving and generating the most up-to-date medical information, providing a valuable aid in decision-making. In content creation, RAG systems can generate high-quality, personalized content that reflects the latest trends, information, and user preferences.

The application of RAG extends beyond specific industries. In **business intelligence**, RAG models are used to synthesize vast amounts of data from different sources, generating reports that are more relevant and insightful. In **education**, RAG systems can be used to generate learning materials tailored to individual student needs, based on real-time data about their progress and preferences. As the technology continues to evolve, the potential for RAG to transform industries by improving the quality and accuracy of AI-generated content is immense.

Looking to the future, the potential for RAG to continue evolving and transforming the landscape of AI text generation is vast.

As AI models become more advanced, the ability to integrate even more dynamic, real-time data into RAG workflows will lead to more personalized, context-aware applications. The continued development of **cross-lingual retrieval** and **multimodal data** (such as combining text with images or audio) will make RAG even more powerful, opening up new possibilities for a wide range of applications. Ultimately, RAG is poised to be a cornerstone in the future of AI, providing tools that will enable businesses, governments, and individuals to harness the power of AI in ways that were once thought impossible.

In summary, Retrieval-Augmented Generation represents a powerful leap forward in AI's ability to generate accurate, relevant, and dynamic text.

By combining the strength of LLMs with real-time data retrieval, RAG systems can produce outputs that are not only contextually aware but also grounded in real, verifiable information. With its application across industries from healthcare to customer service, RAG is not just a trend—it is a transformative technology that will continue to shape the future of AI and text generation.

Chapter 1: Understanding the Basics of RAG: The Architecture

At the core of Retrieval-Augmented Generation (RAG) lies a powerful architecture that seamlessly integrates data retrieval and content generation to produce high-quality, accurate text. Understanding this architecture is key to harnessing the full potential of RAG and its applications in various fields. The architecture is built on two foundational processes: the **retrieval process** and the **generation process**. These two components work in harmony, with each one playing a vital role in producing the desired output.

The **retrieval process** begins with the AI model identifying relevant pieces of information from a vast corpus of data. This step is crucial because the quality of the generated text depends on the quality of the retrieved information. Without accurate, relevant data, the generative model would not be able to produce reliable content. The retrieval process typically involves querying a **vector database**, which stores high-dimensional representations of data points. These vectors allow the system to measure the similarity between a user's input query and the data stored in the database.

Once relevant data is identified, it is passed on to the **generation process**, where the AI model integrates the retrieved information into its output. This stage involves the use of large language models (LLMs) that generate text based on the information provided. The LLM combines the knowledge from the retrieval step with its own internal understanding, creating a response that is both relevant and contextually aware.

This integration of real-time data with the generative capabilities of LLMs is what sets RAG apart from traditional AI systems that rely solely on pre-existing knowledge learned during training.

To fully appreciate how RAG works, it's important to understand the role of **vector databases** in the retrieval process. A vector database is a type of data storage that uses **vectors**—numerical representations of data points—rather than traditional rows and columns. These vectors allow for more sophisticated searches, enabling the system to find and retrieve information based on the **similarity** between the query and the stored data, rather than relying solely on exact keyword matches. This ability to search by similarity makes vector databases highly effective in RAG systems, as they can quickly identify the most relevant data to enhance the generative process.

Vector databases play an integral role in ensuring that the content generated by the AI system is of the highest quality.

Indexing is a critical technique used within these databases to organize the data in such a way that retrieval is efficient and fast. By indexing the data based on the vector representations, the system can quickly access the most relevant information for any given query. This is particularly important when dealing with large datasets, as it ensures that the AI model can access real-time, relevant data without delays.

The **ranking** process further enhances the effectiveness of the retrieval step. Once the data is indexed, it needs to be ranked based on its relevance to the query. This ranking process ensures that the most relevant and useful pieces of information are retrieved and passed on to the generative model. Ranking can be based on a variety of factors, such as the semantic similarity between the query and the data, the recency of the data, or even the credibility of the sources.

By carefully ranking the data, RAG systems can ensure that the AI-generated content is both accurate and relevant, improving the overall user experience.

These processes are made even more effective by integrating advanced **AI models**, such as **BERT**, **GPT-3**, and **T5**, which enhance both retrieval and generation. These models have the ability to understand natural language at a deep level, enabling them to generate text that is contextually rich and aligned with the retrieved information. In RAG systems, these models work hand-in-hand with the retrieval mechanism to produce outputs that are grounded in real-time knowledge while maintaining the coherence and creativity that LLMs are known for.

As AI systems evolve, the architecture behind RAG is becoming increasingly sophisticated, incorporating more complex mechanisms for retrieval and generation.

For example, **fine-tuning** is an important aspect of the generation process, where the AI model is trained further on specialized datasets to improve the quality of the output. In addition, **human feedback loops** are being integrated into RAG workflows, allowing for continuous improvement of the system's performance. By incorporating feedback from users or domain experts, RAG systems can refine their output over time, further enhancing the relevance and accuracy of the generated text.

The combination of efficient retrieval, advanced generation techniques, and the use of vector databases ensures that RAG systems can handle complex tasks with ease. Whether it's generating detailed reports, answering specific queries, or creating personalized content, the architecture behind RAG provides a robust framework for AI-driven content generation.

This architecture makes RAG an indispensable tool for industries ranging from healthcare to finance, where accuracy, speed, and real-time data are critical.

In summary, the architecture of RAG is built on the powerful integration of the **retrieval process** and the **generation process**, supported by the use of vector databases for efficient data retrieval and ranking. The careful design of these systems ensures that RAG-powered AI models can generate high-quality, accurate content that is grounded in real-world data. As the technology continues to evolve, the architecture behind RAG will only become more advanced, opening up new possibilities for AI-driven content creation across industries.

Chapter 2: Preparing the Environment: Tools, Frameworks, and Libraries

Setting up an effective environment for developing Retrieval-Augmented Generation (RAG) systems is crucial for ensuring smooth, efficient workflows. The tools, frameworks, and libraries you choose will form the backbone of your RAG system, enabling you to leverage real-time data and integrate advanced machine learning models into your projects. This section will walk you through the essential components of setting up your development environment, including key frameworks, Python libraries, and hands-on setup tips to get you started with building RAG systems.

One of the most popular and widely used frameworks for RAG systems is **LlamaIndex**. This tool is specifically designed to integrate real-time data retrieval with large language models (LLMs) in an efficient and scalable manner.

By using LlamaIndex, developers can index and retrieve data from various sources, such as document collections, knowledge bases, or APIs, and then pass that data to an LLM for generation. What makes LlamaIndex especially powerful is its ability to handle the complexities of information retrieval while also optimizing for performance. It enables AI systems to generate responses that are both contextually accurate and relevant, by retrieving the most appropriate data points from a vast repository.

Another essential framework in the RAG ecosystem is **Pinecone**. Pinecone is a vector database that allows for fast and scalable retrieval of high-dimensional data. It plays a pivotal role in storing and indexing the vectors that represent the data used in RAG systems.

When working with large datasets, Pinecone's efficiency in searching and retrieving similar data points is invaluable. The power of Pinecone lies in its ability to handle millions of vectors and perform real-time retrieval at scale, making it ideal for use cases where both speed and accuracy are critical. Pinecone integrates seamlessly with LlamaIndex and other tools, making it an essential framework for any RAG system.

In addition to LlamaIndex and Pinecone, **Deep Lake** is another key player in the RAG toolset. Deep Lake is a storage and indexing system designed specifically for large-scale machine learning data. It is optimized for storing and retrieving high-dimensional data, making it an ideal choice for managing the massive volumes of information that RAG systems rely on. Deep Lake offers advanced features for efficiently storing and processing data in ways that are compatible with machine learning workflows.

It's particularly useful when working with multimodal data, as it allows for the seamless integration of text, images, and other forms of data into the retrieval and generation process.

Along with these frameworks, Python libraries play a crucial role in enabling the functionality of RAG systems. One of the most widely used Python libraries in this space is **Transformers**. Developed by Hugging Face, the Transformers library provides access to a wide range of pre-trained models, including some of the most advanced large language models like **GPT**, **BERT**, and **T5**.

These models can be used for both retrieval and generation tasks, and their integration with RAG systems allows for the creation of AI-driven solutions that can generate contextually relevant and highly accurate text. Transformers is designed to be user-friendly, with a vast collection of tools that make it easier for developers to fine-tune and implement LLMs for a variety of use cases.

Another essential library from Hugging Face is **Hugging Face's Datasets** library, which provides access to a large collection of high-quality datasets.

This library is a valuable resource when setting up a RAG system, as it offers datasets that can be used for both training and evaluating models. The Datasets library makes it easy to integrate datasets into your RAG pipeline, whether you're working with text, images, or even structured data. By providing seamless access to a wide variety of datasets, this library helps developers quickly build and optimize their RAG systems without spending excessive time on data collection and preprocessing.

Setting up your **development environment** is the next crucial step in preparing for RAG system development. The environment you choose will depend on the frameworks and libraries you intend to use, but there are several common components that should be part of your setup.

First and foremost, you'll need to install Python and ensure that you have the latest version, as most of the libraries we discussed, including LlamaIndex, Pinecone, and Hugging Face, are Python-based.

Once Python is installed, the next step is setting up a **virtual environment** to manage dependencies. Virtual environments help keep your projects organized by isolating the libraries and dependencies for each project, preventing potential conflicts between different versions. To create a virtual environment, you can use tools like **venv** or **conda**, which are popular choices for managing Python environments. Once your virtual environment is set up, you can install the necessary packages using **pip** or **conda install**, depending on your preference.

To get started with RAG systems, you'll need to install the core frameworks and libraries discussed earlier.

Begin by installing **Transformers** and **Hugging Face** using pip. You can also install **Pinecone** and **Deep Lake** to handle the vector databases and data storage needs of your RAG system. These libraries are well-documented, and the installation processes are straightforward, with comprehensive guides available on their respective websites. It's also recommended to install additional dependencies for handling tasks like data preprocessing, model evaluation, and optimization.

Once your environment is set up, it's time to dive into the **hands-on setup** of your first RAG system. A good place to start is by building a simple retrieval pipeline using **LlamaIndex** and **Pinecone**. You can begin by defining the data sources you want to use, whether they're static datasets, dynamic APIs, or even real-time data from the web. Once the data is indexed and stored in the vector database, you can configure your RAG system to retrieve relevant information based on user input. From there, you'll pass the retrieved data to a pre-trained language model, such as GPT-3 or BERT, to generate contextually accurate responses.

For a complete hands-on project, you can follow these basic steps:

1. **Install the necessary libraries**: Start by installing LlamaIndex, Pinecone, Transformers, and other dependencies.

2. **Set up a vector database**: Use Pinecone or Deep Lake to store and index your data.

3. **Create a retrieval function**: Develop a function that queries the vector database and retrieves the most relevant data based on user input.

4. **Integrate with an LLM**: Use Hugging Face's Transformers library to connect

your RAG system with a pre-trained language model.

5. **Test and iterate**: Run your system through multiple queries to evaluate its performance and accuracy. Make adjustments to the retrieval process, fine-tune the LLM, and optimize the system as necessary.

By following these steps, you'll be able to set up your first RAG system, gaining hands-on experience with the key tools and frameworks involved. As you progress, you can explore more advanced configurations and customizations, refining your system to meet specific needs and performance goals. Whether you're building chatbots, summarization tools, or other generative applications, this hands-on approach will provide you with the foundation needed to succeed in the world of RAG systems.

In summary, preparing the environment for RAG system development involves choosing the right frameworks, libraries, and tools to support your workflow.

By setting up a robust development environment with the necessary dependencies, and getting hands-on with the key components like **LlamaIndex**, **Pinecone**, and **Hugging Face**, you'll be well on your way to building scalable, efficient, and high-performance RAG systems. As you continue to develop your skills, you'll be able to leverage these tools to create more advanced applications that push the boundaries of what's possible with AI-driven content generation.

Chapter 3: Building Your First RAG System: A Hands-On Project

Building your first **Retrieval-Augmented Generation (RAG)** system can be an exciting and rewarding project. By following a step-by-step approach, you'll gain practical insights into the process and understand how RAG systems integrate data retrieval and AI generation for creating highly accurate, contextually aware outputs. This section provides a hands-on guide to building a simple RAG pipeline, including the integration of key frameworks like **LlamaIndex** and **Pinecone**, fine-tuning the AI model for optimal performance, and handling various data types to create a robust and efficient RAG system.

The first step in building your RAG system is setting up a **data retrieval pipeline**. This involves identifying and retrieving the relevant data from an external source, which will then be used to inform the generative model. For this project, you'll integrate **LlamaIndex** and **Pinecone**, two essential tools for indexing and retrieving data efficiently.

Integrating LlamaIndex and Pinecone for Efficient Data Retrieval

LlamaIndex serves as the framework that will allow you to integrate real-time data retrieval into your RAG system. It is designed to efficiently manage and query large datasets, making it an ideal choice for indexing and retrieving information. **Pinecone**, on the other hand, is a powerful vector database that allows for fast and scalable similarity searches. By using Pinecone, you can index the data stored in vector form, which makes retrieving relevant information for your AI model both quick and efficient.

Start by **installing LlamaIndex** and **Pinecone**. These tools can be easily installed via Python's package manager, **pip**. Once installed, the next step is to load the dataset you wish to use for your RAG system. This can be any collection of data, such as text documents, product descriptions, or even APIs. After loading the data, you'll need to **index the content** using Pinecone. This is where the vector database comes into play: it transforms each piece of data into a vector representation, which makes it easier for the system to retrieve relevant content when needed.

With LlamaIndex and Pinecone integrated into your RAG pipeline, the next step is setting up the **retrieval mechanism**. When a user inputs a query, the RAG system will retrieve relevant data by searching Pinecone's vector database. LlamaIndex will manage this process by querying the database and returning the most relevant pieces of information. This process of **retrieving relevant data** forms the first part of your RAG pipeline and is critical for generating accurate and contextually relevant outputs.

Fine-Tuning Your AI Model for Optimal Performance

Once the relevant data is retrieved, the next task is to integrate this information into the generative model. This is where fine-tuning comes into play. Fine-tuning involves adjusting a pre-trained AI model, such as **GPT-3** or **BERT**, to optimize it for your specific use case.

Start by selecting a pre-trained model from a platform like **Hugging Face**. These models have been trained on vast datasets and can generate high-quality text. However, to ensure that the output is relevant to your use case, you'll need to fine-tune the model using the data retrieved from Pinecone. Fine-tuning the model involves adjusting its parameters so it can better understand and generate content that aligns with the specific context of the retrieved data.

Fine-tuning typically requires a **training dataset** that includes examples of the type of output you expect. For example, if you're building a system to generate product descriptions based on retrieved data, you'll need to fine-tune the model with existing product descriptions to help it learn the correct structure and tone. The goal of fine-tuning is to improve the model's ability to generate text that is coherent, contextually accurate, and aligned with the information retrieved by the system.

The next step in the fine-tuning process is **hyperparameter optimization**. This involves adjusting settings such as the learning rate, batch size, and number of training epochs to ensure that the model learns efficiently without overfitting or underfitting. Hyperparameter optimization can be done manually or through automated tools, such as **GridSearch** or **RandomSearch**, to find the best configuration for your use case.

Handling Text Data and Real-Time Data Retrieval

Once your model is fine-tuned, it's time to handle the data that will be processed by your RAG system. RAG systems typically work with **text data**, but you may also need to handle **real-time data**. Real-time data retrieval is especially important for applications like chatbots, customer support, or news summarization, where the information must be up-to-date.

To handle text data, ensure that your RAG system can properly preprocess and clean the input data before passing it to the model. This includes tasks like tokenization, removing stop words, and normalizing the text. It's also important to ensure that the data is in a format that is compatible with the vector database. Once the data is preprocessed, it can be indexed by Pinecone, allowing the system to retrieve relevant information when prompted.

When it comes to **real-time data retrieval**, your system will need to be capable of fetching the most current information as the user interacts with it. For instance, if you are building a RAG system for **stock market analysis**, the system should be able to pull in the latest stock data in real time and use it to inform the AI-generated responses. This requires setting up a **data pipeline** that connects to external APIs, news sources, or databases, and updates the knowledge base with fresh information regularly.

Troubleshooting Common Issues

As with any complex system, you may encounter issues while building your RAG pipeline. Here are some common issues and how to address them:

1. **Retrieval Issues**: If the system fails to retrieve relevant data, it may be due to problems with the vector database indexing or poor-quality data. To resolve

this, check the indexing process to ensure that the data is represented correctly in vector format. You may also need to fine-tune the retrieval parameters, such as the similarity threshold, to improve the quality of the results.

2. **Model Generation Issues**: If the AI model generates irrelevant or incoherent text, the issue may lie in the fine-tuning process. Ensure that the model has been fine-tuned on a dataset that closely aligns with the type of output you expect. If necessary, adjust the hyperparameters to improve the model's learning process.

3. **Data Formatting Issues**: Sometimes, the data retrieved by the system may not be in the correct format for processing. This can cause errors during the generation process. To resolve this,

ensure that the data is properly cleaned and formatted before being passed to the model.

4. **Performance Issues**: If your RAG system is slow or lagging, consider optimizing the performance by reducing the size of the vector database or implementing caching techniques to store frequently retrieved data. You can also optimize the model's processing speed by using smaller models or leveraging hardware accelerators, such as GPUs or TPUs.

In summary, building your first RAG system is a step-by-step process that involves integrating data retrieval with text generation, fine-tuning AI models, and handling real-time data. By following the steps outlined above and addressing common issues along the way, you'll be well on your way to creating a fully functional RAG system. Whether you're building chatbots, content generation tools, or more complex applications, the principles and techniques covered here provide a solid foundation for leveraging RAG technology to create high-quality, contextually aware AI outputs.

Chapter 4: Data Retrieval Techniques: Optimizing for Accuracy and Speed

In the world of Retrieval-Augmented Generation (RAG), **data retrieval** is a pivotal step in ensuring that the AI systems produce accurate, contextually relevant, and fast responses. The success of your RAG system depends on how well the system can retrieve the right data from vast, dynamic datasets. This section delves into the advanced techniques for optimizing data retrieval, including **indexing**, **chunking**, and optimizing query responses to ensure both **speed** and **accuracy**. It also covers strategies for handling **real-time data**, which is essential for applications that require up-to-date information.

Advanced Data Retrieval: Techniques for Indexing, Chunking, and Optimizing Query Responses

When it comes to **indexing**, the first step is to organize the data in a way that allows the retrieval system to quickly find and access relevant pieces of information.

Without proper indexing, retrieving accurate data from large datasets can be inefficient, and retrieval times can become prohibitively slow. Effective indexing involves creating **vector representations** of the data, which is where **vector databases** like **Pinecone** and **Deep Lake** come into play. These databases store data as vectors, allowing the retrieval process to focus on finding similarities rather than exact matches.

One of the most commonly used techniques for indexing is **inverted indexing**, which involves creating a reverse index of terms that appear in your data and mapping them to the document or data source they belong to. This allows for a fast search of relevant documents when a query is issued.

The key here is ensuring that the **inverted index** is optimized, meaning it should be regularly updated and refined as new data is added to the system. This can be done by adding or removing entries based on relevance and importance.

Once the data is indexed, **chunking** comes into play. Chunking involves breaking down large pieces of text or data into smaller, more manageable segments that can be processed more efficiently. When working with large datasets, especially those involving long-form text or complex data structures, chunking allows the retrieval system to search smaller, more focused segments, significantly speeding up the retrieval process. The goal is to break the data into chunks that are contextually meaningful and contain enough information to answer potential queries.

For instance, when dealing with large documents like research papers or product manuals, chunking allows the system to pull only the most relevant paragraphs or sections. By **optimizing chunk sizes**, you can strike a balance between too large chunks that contain too much irrelevant data and too small chunks that may not provide enough context. This fine-tuning helps improve the accuracy of data retrieval, ensuring that the most relevant and complete pieces of information are returned to the generative model for further processing.

In addition to chunking, **query optimization** plays a critical role in enhancing retrieval accuracy and speed. Query optimization involves refining the way queries are processed and matched against indexed data. One key aspect of query optimization is using **semantic search** techniques, which involve matching queries with data that is conceptually similar rather than relying solely on keyword matches.

Semantic search is powered by **embedding models** that convert text into dense vector representations, allowing the system to better understand the meaning of the query and the data being retrieved.

To further optimize query responses, you can implement **ranking mechanisms** that prioritize the most relevant documents or data segments based on specific criteria, such as **semantic similarity**, **recency**, or **relevance** to the user's query. **Re-ranking** is also an important technique, where the system re-evaluates and adjusts the retrieved results based on additional criteria or feedback from the generative model itself. This fine-tuned ranking system helps ensure that only the best possible responses are passed on for further processing.

Handling Real-Time Data: Strategies for Ensuring AI Systems Can Retrieve Relevant Data in Real Time

One of the significant advantages of RAG systems is their ability to retrieve and integrate **real-time data**, making them highly effective in dynamic, fast-changing environments. This is particularly important in applications such as **financial analysis**, **news summarization**, **customer service**, or **stock market prediction**, where accurate and up-to-date information is essential for generating reliable outputs.

Real-time data retrieval requires a different approach from traditional data retrieval systems, as the data must be continuously updated and processed in real time. To ensure that your AI system can handle real-time data, it's crucial to implement a system that can continuously **monitor data sources** for changes and updates. This can be achieved by setting up **data pipelines** that automatically pull in the latest information from relevant sources such as APIs, web scraping, or real-time data feeds.

For example, in the case of stock market prediction, the system should be able to pull in the latest stock prices, news, and trading volumes in real time to make accurate predictions.

One technique for managing real-time data is **streaming data ingestion**, where data is fed into the system continuously, rather than in large batches. This allows the system to process data as it arrives, ensuring that it's always working with the most current information. In this setup, real-time data is typically stored in **circular buffers** or **time-series databases**, which are optimized for handling high-frequency data streams. These tools are capable of storing data for short periods of time and are well-suited to applications that require fast retrieval and processing of real-time information.

Another crucial aspect of real-time data retrieval is **data freshness**. Depending on the application, the freshness of the data may be more important than the absolute accuracy.

For example, in **real-time news summarization**, the goal is to pull in the latest headlines and generate summaries quickly, even if the information is not as deeply validated as in other applications. To achieve this, the system must be designed to prioritize speed over exhaustive data checking, retrieving the most recent information as quickly as possible.

Moreover, to handle the challenge of retrieving **relevant real-time data**, RAG systems should integrate **dynamic retrieval mechanisms**. These mechanisms help the system adjust its search and retrieval strategies based on the current context. For instance, if a system is retrieving data for a customer support query, it may prioritize responses from recent conversations or knowledge base updates, while for a financial analysis application, it may prioritize the latest market trends or stock prices.

This requires the system to be context-aware and adaptive, ensuring that the data retrieved aligns with the immediate needs of the user.

Finally, **scalability** is a critical consideration for handling real-time data. As the volume of data increases, the system must be able to scale without losing performance. This can be achieved by distributing the data across multiple servers or using **cloud-based solutions** that provide elastic scalability. Cloud platforms like **AWS**, **Google Cloud**, and **Azure** offer tools for handling large amounts of data in real time, ensuring that your RAG system can scale efficiently as the amount of incoming data grows.

In summary, optimizing data retrieval in RAG systems involves advanced techniques like indexing, chunking, and query optimization to ensure fast and accurate responses. For real-time data handling, implementing data pipelines, streaming data ingestion, and dynamic retrieval mechanisms is essential for ensuring that AI systems can provide accurate, up-to-date information. By refining these processes, you can build a RAG system that not only retrieves relevant data but does so quickly and efficiently, providing high-quality AI outputs in real-time applications.

Chapter 5: Advanced RAG Techniques: Scaling and Customizing Your System

As Retrieval-Augmented Generation (RAG) systems continue to evolve, scaling and customizing these systems have become crucial for achieving greater accuracy, reliability, and adaptability across a wide range of applications. Scaling RAG systems allows them to handle large datasets efficiently, while customization enables businesses to tailor the system's retrieval and generation capabilities to their specific needs. This chapter delves into the strategies for scaling your RAG system, ensuring that it remains robust and efficient even as the size and complexity of the dataset grow. It also explores how you can customize the retrieval process to meet specific business requirements, such as integrating **human**

feedback to enhance the system's performance and output accuracy.

Scaling Your RAG System: Handling Large Datasets and Increasing Robustness

Scaling a RAG system to handle large datasets is an essential challenge for any application that needs to process vast amounts of information quickly and accurately. Whether you're working with **massive collections of documents**, **real-time data streams**, or **multimodal datasets**, ensuring that the retrieval and generation process can scale effectively is critical to maintaining performance.

The first step in scaling your RAG system is ensuring that the **data retrieval pipeline** is optimized for large volumes of data. One effective technique for handling large datasets is **distributed indexing**. Rather than storing the entire dataset in a single database or server, distributed indexing spreads the dataset across multiple nodes, allowing for parallel processing. This enables faster searches and retrievals, especially when dealing with datasets that can no longer be stored or processed on a single machine. Distributed vector databases like **Pinecone** or **Deep Lake** can be used in this context to spread data across different storage units, enhancing retrieval speed and ensuring the system remains responsive as the dataset expands.

Next, consider leveraging **sharding** for further optimization. Sharding is the process of splitting data into smaller, more manageable chunks or "shards," which can be stored across multiple servers. This approach minimizes bottlenecks and allows each shard to be processed independently. For example, if your dataset includes multiple types of data, such as text, images, and audio, you can shard the data by type, processing each shard separately but in parallel. This ensures that the system can scale effectively, even as the dataset grows exponentially.

Another strategy for scaling RAG systems is **caching**. Caching involves storing frequently accessed data in fast-access memory, such as **RAM** or **SSD storage**, to reduce the time it takes to retrieve commonly used information. For example, if your system is frequently querying the same documents or sources, caching can store those results so they can be retrieved instantly. This technique significantly reduces latency and improves overall system performance. However, caching requires careful management to ensure that outdated data is not served, especially when working with **real-time data** that may change frequently.

Load balancing is another important strategy for scaling. Load balancing ensures that the processing power of the system is evenly distributed across multiple servers or machines. This prevents any single machine from becoming overwhelmed, thus maintaining the responsiveness and stability of the system. By distributing requests across a set of servers, load balancing ensures that your RAG system can scale horizontally, supporting greater volumes of traffic and data without compromising performance.

Finally, to ensure the system remains **robust** as it scales, implementing **monitoring and logging** systems is essential. Continuous monitoring of system performance—such as query times, response accuracy, and resource usage—enables you to identify potential issues before they impact the user experience. Setting up automated alerts for performance degradation allows for timely intervention and ensures the system's robustness at scale.

Customizing Retrieval: Tailoring the Retrieval Process to Specific Business Needs

While scaling ensures that a RAG system can handle large amounts of data, **customizing** the retrieval process is essential for tailoring the system to specific business needs. Customization allows businesses to fine-tune how data is retrieved, ensuring that the system prioritizes the most relevant and contextually appropriate information.

One of the first steps in customizing the retrieval process is **prioritizing certain data sources**. Depending on the nature of your business, some sources of data may be more important or relevant than others. For example, in a **customer service application**, the system might prioritize retrieving information from a company's most frequently accessed support documents or FAQ pages. In contrast, a **financial forecasting system** may give preference to real-time stock market data, economic reports, and financial news.

Customizing the retrieval process involves setting up rules or priorities that ensure the most relevant data sources are queried first.

Another key aspect of customization is **tailoring the similarity search** to better match the needs of your business.

By using **semantic search** techniques, you can refine how the system matches queries to the most relevant data. For example, instead of relying on exact keyword matching, you can use **vector embeddings** to match queries with data that has a similar meaning, even if the words don't match exactly. This is especially important for complex or ambiguous queries, where semantic understanding is necessary to retrieve the most relevant results.

Personalization is another critical area of customization. Personalization ensures that the system retrieves information that is specifically relevant to individual users. In customer-facing applications, this could involve adjusting the retrieval process to prioritize data based on a user's previous interactions, preferences, or browsing history.

For instance, in a **content recommendation system**, the RAG model can retrieve content recommendations that are personalized to a user's tastes, pulling in relevant articles, videos, or products based on past preferences.

In addition to these techniques, **incorporating human feedback** into the retrieval process is an effective way to improve the accuracy and relevance of the results. As AI systems can sometimes retrieve irrelevant or incomplete data, integrating **feedback loops** can refine the retrieval process over time. By allowing users or domain experts to correct or validate retrieved information, the system learns to prioritize more accurate and relevant sources in the future. Feedback mechanisms can be incorporated into the system by using a **reinforcement learning** approach, where the system is rewarded for making accurate data retrievals and penalized for poor ones.

Moreover, integrating **dynamic retrieval strategies** is essential for systems that need to adapt to changing data. A dynamic retrieval system can adjust its search criteria based on factors such as the user's query history, context, or even external data sources. For example, a **real-time news summarization system** may prioritize recent news articles over older ones, adjusting the retrieval parameters to ensure the most up-to-date information is used to generate summaries.

Finally, **adaptive filtering** is an advanced technique that can further enhance the customization of the retrieval process. Adaptive filtering allows the system to learn from user behavior and continuously adjust its retrieval approach. For example, if users tend to favor certain types of content or data sources, the system can prioritize those sources over time, improving the relevance of future queries.

In conclusion, scaling and customizing a RAG system are key to maximizing its effectiveness in real-world applications. Scaling ensures that your system can handle larger datasets efficiently by implementing techniques such as distributed indexing, sharding, caching, and load balancing.

Customization, on the other hand, enables businesses to tailor the retrieval process to specific needs, ensuring that the system prioritizes the most relevant data and adapts over time. By fine-tuning the retrieval mechanisms, integrating **human feedback**, and implementing dynamic strategies, you can ensure that your RAG system remains highly accurate, relevant, and scalable, providing valuable insights across a wide range of industries and applications.

Chapter 6: Multimodal RAG: Integrating Text, Images, and Other Data Types

---

Multimodal Retrieval-Augmented Generation (RAG) represents a significant advancement in artificial intelligence, enabling systems to integrate and process multiple forms of data—such as text, images, audio, and even video—to generate richer, more context-aware responses. By incorporating these various data types, multimodal RAG systems have the potential to enhance decision-making processes, improve user interactions, and create more intuitive and effective AI-driven applications.

In this chapter, we will explore the capabilities of multimodal RAG, discussing how it works and how it can be applied across industries like healthcare, retail, and more.

Multimodal Capabilities: Integrating Text, Images, and Other Data Types for More Context-Aware AI Responses

Traditionally, AI systems have primarily relied on text data for generating responses or making decisions. However, the real world is multimodal in nature, and valuable insights are often hidden across different types of data. For example, a medical diagnosis might require not only a description of symptoms (text) but also imaging data such as X-rays or MRIs. Similarly, in retail, customer preferences can be derived not just from textual reviews but also from images of the products, as well as audio feedback in customer service interactions.

Multimodal RAG systems go beyond the limitations of text-based systems by incorporating a multi-input approach, where different data types are integrated to inform the AI model.

The system can retrieve relevant information from a combination of textual content, images, and other data forms and use this information to generate a more accurate, relevant, and contextually aware output. For example, a multimodal RAG model might retrieve text descriptions of products, images of the products themselves, and customer audio reviews to generate a detailed and personalized recommendation for a user.

The integration of these different data types requires specialized models and techniques. Text data is typically processed using traditional language models like GPT-3 or BERT, while images are processed using convolutional neural networks (CNNs) or other computer vision models. The challenge lies in combining these data streams in a way that allows the model to understand how they relate to one another.

The system must not only retrieve the most relevant text and images but also understand the context in which these different types of data interact. This can be achieved through techniques such as cross-modal embeddings, where text and image data are converted into a common representation, allowing them to be compared and processed together.

For example, if you are building a RAG system for a fashion e-commerce platform, the system could retrieve a product description (text), an image of the product, and user reviews (text and images), then generate a product recommendation based on the combined context of these data points. The text data helps the system understand the product's features, while the image gives it a visual sense of the product's appearance, and the reviews provide social proof and customer feedback.

The process of combining these modalities effectively involves several steps. First, each modality must be encoded into a common format that can be processed by the AI model. Text data is typically converted into word embeddings or tokenized sequences, while images are transformed into feature vectors using computer vision techniques. Once the data is encoded, it is passed through the RAG system, where retrieval and generation processes are performed based on the integrated information.

One of the significant advantages of multimodal RAG is the ability to create more robust and accurate responses. For example, a multimodal RAG system in healthcare could not only retrieve relevant clinical notes (text) but also analyze medical images like X-rays or CT scans (visual data) to provide a more accurate diagnosis or recommendation. This makes the system far more powerful and contextually aware than a traditional text-based system, allowing it to draw on a wider range of information.

Applications Across Industries: How Multimodal RAG Enhances Decision-Making and Customer Interaction

Multimodal RAG is already transforming a range of industries by improving decision-making and creating more engaging customer experiences. Here, we will examine how multimodal RAG is applied in healthcare, retail, and other fields, showcasing its potential to enhance AI-driven applications.

Healthcare: Improving Diagnostics and Decision Support

In the healthcare industry, multimodal RAG has immense potential to improve decision-making and patient care. A traditional AI system might only process text data, such as medical records or clinical notes. However, in healthcare, relevant information often exists in various forms—text, images, and even audio (e.g., voice recordings from consultations). Multimodal RAG systems can combine these data types to generate more accurate diagnoses, treatment recommendations, and personalized care plans.

For example, in radiology, a multimodal RAG system can analyze medical images like X-rays, CT scans, and MRI scans, and combine this visual data with relevant patient records (text) to make diagnostic suggestions.

The system can retrieve medical history, lab results, and research papers (text data), cross-reference them with the visual data from the scans, and provide more accurate insights. The added benefit of using multimodal RAG in healthcare is its ability to process real-time data from medical devices, helping doctors make faster and more informed decisions.

This technology can also be used in telemedicine. For instance, a multimodal RAG system can analyze video consultations (audio-visual data) and combine them with the patient's medical history (text) to provide real-time suggestions for treatment or next steps.

By combining text, image, and audio data, healthcare professionals can rely on a more comprehensive tool for diagnostic support, reducing errors and improving patient outcomes.

Retail: Personalizing Customer Experiences

In the retail sector, multimodal RAG is transforming how businesses interact with customers and personalize their shopping experiences. Online retailers can use multimodal RAG systems to enhance their recommendation engines by integrating data from multiple sources. For example, consider a fashion retailer that wants to recommend clothing items to customers.

A multimodal RAG system can retrieve text-based product descriptions, user reviews, and images of clothing, as well as audio feedback from customer service interactions, to provide tailored product recommendations.

The system can also combine visual and textual data to improve the search experience. For example, a customer could search for a specific style of clothing, and the system could retrieve both image-based data (pictures of clothing) and text-based data (product descriptions) to find the most relevant matches. This integration of multiple modalities allows the system to better understand customer preferences, leading to more personalized suggestions and enhanced customer satisfaction.

In customer support, multimodal RAG systems can process customer service tickets or live chats (text), voice interactions (audio), and even product images submitted by customers to provide faster, more accurate responses. Whether it's troubleshooting a product issue or guiding a customer through a process, the combination of text, image, and audio data helps the system generate responses that are more contextually aware and relevant.

Other Industries: Enhancing Decision Support and Information Retrieval

Beyond healthcare and retail, multimodal RAG can be applied across various industries to enhance decision support and improve information retrieval. In manufacturing, for example, a multimodal RAG system could combine text-based maintenance manuals with images of machine parts or even video tutorials to provide technicians with more accurate guidance on repairs. In legal fields, multimodal systems can analyze court case documents (text) and legal precedents (text), as well as incorporate images of legal documents, to generate more informed legal opinions or case analysis.

In education, multimodal RAG can be used to create more dynamic and personalized learning experiences. By combining text, video lectures, and interactive visual content, educational platforms can generate learning materials that adapt to the student's learning style and current progress. For instance, a multimodal RAG system might retrieve relevant textbook chapters, videos, and interactive exercises based on a student's quiz results and learning history, ensuring a more engaging and effective educational experience.

Multimodal RAG is an exciting frontier in AI technology, providing systems that are not only more context-aware but also capable of handling diverse data types to generate richer, more relevant outputs. By integrating text, images, and other forms of data, multimodal RAG systems can significantly improve decision-making and enhance customer interactions across a wide range of industries. Whether in healthcare, retail, education, or other fields, the ability to process and retrieve information from multiple sources in real-time is unlocking new possibilities for more dynamic and personalized AI applications.

As this technology continues to develop, it will undoubtedly play a key role in shaping the future of AI-driven solutions.

Chapter 7: Ethics and Bias in RAG: Ensuring Fair and Transparent AI Systems

As the adoption of **Retrieval-Augmented Generation (RAG)** continues to grow, ensuring that AI systems operate ethically and fairly has become a central concern. RAG systems, like all AI technologies, must be built with strong ethical principles at their core, ensuring that the outputs they generate are not only accurate but also transparent and free from harmful biases. The need for **ethical AI** in the development and deployment of RAG systems is paramount, as these technologies are increasingly integrated into applications that impact people's lives, such as healthcare, finance, and customer service.

This chapter will explore the key aspects of ethical AI, offering practical guidance on building RAG systems that are fair, transparent, and responsible. Additionally, we will discuss the challenges of **bias in AI models** and provide actionable steps to minimize these biases, ensuring that RAG systems produce outputs that are both equitable and accurate.

Ethical AI: Building Fair, Transparent, and Responsible RAG Systems

Creating ethical AI systems is not just about achieving technical excellence; it also involves **building trust** with users and stakeholders. In the context of RAG, ethical AI requires addressing the inherent risks associated with using AI to generate and retrieve information from vast datasets. Ethical concerns around data privacy, algorithmic accountability, and transparency are essential when developing RAG systems, especially when these systems are making decisions that affect real-world outcomes.

A fundamental aspect of **ethical AI** in RAG systems is ensuring **transparency**. Transparency refers to the ability of users to understand how the AI system operates, how it retrieves and generates content, and how it reaches conclusions.

For a RAG system to be transparent, it should provide clear insights into the **data sources** it uses for retrieval and generation, including whether the data is updated in real-time and where it comes from. For example, in a **healthcare application**, transparency ensures that doctors and patients understand the origins of the medical information provided by the system—whether it is based on verified research, clinical notes, or real-time data from medical devices.

Another key principle of ethical AI is **accountability**. Developers and organizations must ensure that they are accountable for the AI systems they build and deploy.

This includes documenting the design decisions made during the development of the RAG system, such as which datasets are used for training and retrieval, and how the system's outputs are evaluated for accuracy and fairness. **Accountability** also involves creating mechanisms for users to challenge or question the AI's decisions, ensuring that there is always an avenue for oversight and correction if necessary.

To ensure that RAG systems are **fair**, developers must work to eliminate discrimination or favoritism in the system's outputs. Fairness in AI involves designing systems that do not perpetuate or exacerbate existing social inequalities, such as biases based on race, gender, or socioeconomic status. For example, a RAG system used in **job recruitment** should not favor candidates from specific demographic groups or perpetuate historical biases.

Achieving fairness requires careful consideration of the data being used to train the models, ensuring that the data does not contain inherent biases that could lead to biased or discriminatory outputs.

Moreover, ethical AI calls for **privacy protection**. RAG systems often retrieve and generate sensitive data, such as medical records, financial information, or personal identifiers. It is essential to ensure that these systems are compliant with privacy regulations such as the **General Data Protection Regulation (GDPR)** or the **Health Insurance Portability and Accountability Act (HIPAA)** in the U.S. Privacy considerations must be baked into the design of the system from the outset, including ensuring that sensitive data is anonymized, encrypted, and used in a way that respects individuals' rights to privacy.

Bias Mitigation: Practical Steps to Ensure RAG Models Produce Unbiased Outputs

Bias in AI systems, including RAG models, is a well-documented issue that can arise from multiple sources. The **data** used to train or retrieve information can contain biases, either from historical inequities or from skewed representations in the data itself. These biases can then propagate through the AI system, leading to outputs that reflect and reinforce these biases. Bias in RAG systems can have significant consequences, especially when the outputs are used to make decisions in areas like hiring, lending, or healthcare, where fairness is critical.

To mitigate bias, the first step is to **carefully curate and audit the data** used for both the retrieval and generative components of the RAG system. This involves evaluating datasets for potential **biases** related to gender, race, age, and other social factors.

If a dataset is found to have significant biases, the next step is to either **remove** or **balance** the data. For example, if a healthcare dataset predominantly includes data from one demographic group, it may be necessary to augment the dataset with data from underrepresented groups to ensure that the model learns from a more diverse set of examples.

The **choice of data sources** used in retrieval is just as important. RAG systems rely heavily on external data sources, which can often introduce biases depending on the quality and nature of the source. For example, a RAG system retrieving information from biased or outdated websites may produce skewed or inaccurate results. It is important to establish clear guidelines for selecting reliable, diverse, and **ethically sound sources** for the data that the RAG system will retrieve.

Another critical step in bias mitigation is **fine-tuning the generative model** to improve its accuracy and fairness.

Fine-tuning involves adjusting the model's parameters to reduce bias, based on a more diverse and representative training dataset. Techniques like **adversarial training** can be used, where a second model is trained to detect and mitigate bias in the outputs generated by the main model. The goal of fine-tuning is not only to make the system more accurate but also to ensure that it treats all demographic groups fairly and equitably.

Bias detection and testing should also be integrated into the development process. Regularly testing the RAG system for biased outputs is essential, as even small biases in the data can result in disproportionately large impacts when scaled. One effective method of detecting bias is to use **fairness metrics** to assess the system's outputs.

These metrics can help identify whether the model is treating different groups equally or if there are disparities in the results. It's also useful to conduct regular **human audits** to evaluate the system's outputs, ensuring that they align with ethical standards and reflect fairness in decision-making.

In addition to **data and model adjustments**, **feedback loops** play an essential role in mitigating bias. By incorporating feedback from diverse users and stakeholders, developers can continuously refine and improve the system to ensure that it performs equitably across all contexts. For example, feedback from end-users can help identify if certain groups are systematically disadvantaged by the AI's outputs. In this way, feedback loops help RAG systems evolve and become more responsible over time.

Ensuring Responsible Use of RAG Systems

Finally, ensuring that RAG systems are used **responsibly** is a shared responsibility between developers, businesses, and end-users.

Developers must ensure that the systems they create adhere to ethical guidelines and fairness standards, while businesses deploying these systems must use them in ways that are transparent, accountable, and consistent with ethical principles. To support responsible use, businesses should establish clear **policies and guidelines** for how RAG systems are to be used, ensuring that they do not reinforce harmful biases or make decisions that could negatively impact certain individuals or groups.

Furthermore, **ongoing monitoring** of RAG systems in the field is necessary to ensure they continue to operate in an ethical and responsible manner. This includes monitoring the system's performance, evaluating the fairness of its outputs, and updating the system as new data or ethical guidelines emerge.

Ethics and bias mitigation are not afterthoughts in the development of RAG systems—they must be integral to the design and deployment process.

By building AI systems that are transparent, accountable, and fair, developers can ensure that their systems operate in ways that respect individual rights and promote equity. Furthermore, by actively addressing bias through data auditing, model fine-tuning, fairness testing, and human feedback loops, RAG systems can generate responsible outputs that benefit society as a whole. As we continue to integrate AI into decision-making processes across various industries, ensuring that these systems are ethical and free from bias will be essential in fostering trust and accountability in AI technologies.

Chapter 8: Cost and Performance Management: Optimizing Your RAG Systems

---

When developing and deploying Retrieval-Augmented Generation (RAG) systems, optimizing for both performance and cost is essential. As RAG systems scale to handle larger datasets and more complex tasks, the need for efficient performance tuning becomes more critical to maintain fast response times while ensuring the accuracy of the outputs. At the same time, managing the costs of running these systems—especially when utilizing large-scale data storage, real-time retrieval, and advanced generative models—becomes a key consideration.

This chapter will explore techniques for improving the performance of RAG systems while maintaining high-quality results.

Additionally, it will provide cost optimization strategies to help developers reduce operational expenses without sacrificing system reliability and accuracy.

Performance Tuning: Balancing Retrieval Speed, Cost, and Accuracy

Performance tuning is all about ensuring that your RAG system is both fast and accurate. When working with large-scale datasets and complex models, the performance of the system can be compromised in several ways, such as slow retrieval times, inefficient use of resources, or the generation of irrelevant or incorrect content. To optimize performance, it's important to balance retrieval speed, cost, and accuracy.

Optimizing Retrieval Speed

One of the key areas where performance tuning is critical is in the retrieval process. In RAG systems, retrieval speed directly impacts how quickly relevant data can be fetched from databases, indexed, and processed by the AI model. If retrieval is slow, it will bottleneck the entire system, leading to delays and longer response times.

A critical technique for improving retrieval speed is vector optimization. When using vector databases like Pinecone or Deep Lake, indexing and storing data in high-dimensional vector spaces can be highly efficient, but it also requires careful optimization. For instance, the use of approximate nearest neighbor (ANN) search can significantly reduce retrieval times by prioritizing speed over the exhaustive search for the most exact matches. By using ANN algorithms like HNSW (Hierarchical Navigable Small World) or IVF (Inverted File), you can speed up the retrieval process without compromising the accuracy of the results.

Additionally, batch retrieval is a technique that can improve performance when handling multiple requests at once. Instead of processing each query individually, batching queries together allows the system to retrieve several data points simultaneously, which can save significant time and resources when working with high-throughput systems.

Balancing Cost and Retrieval Performance

While optimizing for speed, it's important to consider the cost of running large-scale RAG systems. Faster retrieval often requires more computational power, whether that's through the use of specialized hardware (e.g., GPUs, TPUs) or by maintaining large, distributed systems. While these technologies can significantly enhance performance, they also come with a higher price tag.

To balance cost and performance, consider cost-effective retrieval strategies such as data pruning and query caching. Data pruning involves reducing the dataset size by removing outdated, redundant, or irrelevant data from the index. This helps speed up retrieval times by limiting the amount of information the system needs to sift through. Regularly cleaning up your data storage can also reduce the operational costs of maintaining large datasets.

Query caching involves storing frequently requested data in fast-access memory (e.g., RAM or SSD). By caching responses to common or repeated queries, the system can serve these requests without having to perform a new retrieval operation, thereby reducing the computational load and speeding up response times. This strategy is particularly effective in environments where users frequently ask similar questions or request the same information.

Optimizing Generative Model Performance

The generation phase of RAG systems—where the retrieved data is processed and used by an

AI model to generate text—also impacts overall performance. To optimize generation performance, you need to focus on model efficiency and fine-tuning.

For example, using smaller, more efficient models can help reduce response times and resource consumption, especially when processing queries that don't require the full complexity of larger models. For tasks where contextual depth is important but real-time performance is a priority, models like DistilBERT or ALBERT (smaller, optimized versions of BERT) can provide an effective balance between speed and accuracy.

Fine-tuning also plays a role in improving performance. By training the generative model specifically on the types of data it will handle—whether it's product descriptions, medical records, or news articles—you can reduce the number of computations needed to generate relevant responses.

Transfer learning can be used to adapt pre-trained models to specialized tasks, reducing the amount of time and computational power required for training.

Cost Optimization: Reducing Costs While Maintaining High-Quality Performance

Running a large-scale RAG system can be expensive, particularly when dealing with data storage, model training, and real-time processing. However, there are several strategies to optimize costs while ensuring high-quality performance.

Efficient Data Storage and Retrieval

One of the largest expenses in any RAG system is data storage, particularly when dealing with large datasets that need to be indexed and retrieved in real time. Using cloud-based storage solutions like AWS S3, Google Cloud Storage, or Azure Blob Storage can help you reduce costs by only paying for the storage you need, without the need to invest in expensive hardware. These platforms also offer scalability, allowing you to expand or reduce storage as your needs change.

To further reduce costs, consider data compression techniques, which can reduce the size of your datasets while maintaining the integrity of the information. Lossless compression can shrink the data size without losing any important information, which can significantly lower storage costs without compromising the quality of your retrieval process.

Utilizing Pre-trained Models and Efficient Infrastructure

Model training can be one of the most expensive aspects of building and maintaining a RAG system. Training large language models or fine-tuning them on your specific dataset requires a substantial amount of computational power and time. To optimize for cost, consider using pre-trained models available through platforms like Hugging Face. These models are already trained on massive datasets and can be fine-tuned to your specific needs, saving you the time and resources required to train from scratch.

For large-scale systems, consider using cloud-based machine learning infrastructure (such as AWS SageMaker, Google AI Platform, or Azure Machine Learning). These platforms allow you to scale your processing power up or down based on demand, ensuring that you only pay for what you need when you need it. Additionally, cloud platforms offer access to TPUs and GPUs—specialized hardware that can significantly speed up model training and inference times—while providing pay-as-you-go pricing to help control costs.

Model and Query Optimization

Optimizing models and queries can directly impact computational costs. One way to reduce the cost of AI inference (the process of generating responses from trained models) is by using model distillation techniques. Distillation involves creating smaller, more efficient models that retain much of the performance of larger models. These smaller models can process queries faster and with fewer computational resources, reducing inference costs without sacrificing accuracy.

Similarly, query optimization is another area where costs can be controlled. By reducing the complexity of queries or limiting the scope of searches, you can decrease the amount of data that needs to be processed and retrieved. Fine-tuning the retrieval system to limit the amount of information queried, and using query filters to narrow results, helps speed up the system while keeping costs in check.

Monitoring and Continuous Optimization

To ensure that your RAG system is always running at optimal performance and cost, set up monitoring tools to track resource usage, processing times, and costs. Tools like Prometheus, Grafana, or CloudWatch allow you to monitor the performance of your system in real time, providing insights into where inefficiencies are occurring and helping you make data-driven decisions about where to optimize.

Regularly evaluate your system's performance by testing different configurations and evaluating the trade-offs between cost, performance, and accuracy. Continuously tweaking your system based on usage patterns and performance data can help you maintain a cost-effective solution without compromising the quality of the output.

Optimizing the performance and costs of your RAG system is an ongoing process that requires careful consideration of factors such as data storage, retrieval speed, model efficiency, and computational resources. By implementing strategies like vector optimization, query caching, model distillation, and cloud-based infrastructure, you can significantly improve the system's performance while maintaining cost efficiency.

The key is finding a balance between speed, accuracy, and cost, ensuring that your RAG system remains both high-performing and affordable as it scales. Through continuous monitoring and optimization, you can ensure that your RAG system delivers valuable, accurate insights without breaking the budget.

Chapter 9: Deploying Your RAG System: From Development to Production

---

Deploying a Retrieval-Augmented Generation (RAG) system is a critical step that bridges the gap between development and real-world applications. The deployment process involves taking the model and system built in the development phase and ensuring that it functions effectively in a production environment, where real-time data retrieval, scaling, and constant updates are crucial. This chapter explores the best practices for deploying RAG systems, focusing on utilizing cloud platforms for scaling and ensuring that the system operates efficiently.

Additionally, we will discuss the importance of system monitoring to keep your RAG system performing optimally as it moves from development to production.

Deployment: Best Practices for Deploying RAG Systems

Deploying a RAG system requires careful planning to ensure that it can handle the demands of a production environment, including real-time data retrieval, high query volumes, and performance at scale. The goal is to create a system that not only performs well under heavy load but also integrates smoothly with external data sources and applications.

Choosing the Right Cloud Platform for Deployment

When deploying a RAG system, cloud platforms are often the best choice due to their scalability, flexibility, and access to powerful tools and resources. Cloud platforms like Amazon Web Services (AWS), Google Cloud Platform (GCP), and Microsoft Azure offer robust infrastructure for deploying AI models, managing large datasets, and performing real-time data retrieval.

One of the first decisions when deploying your RAG system is choosing between different cloud services that suit the specific needs of your system.

For example, AWS offers a wide range of services for AI and machine learning, including SageMaker for building and deploying models, Lambda for serverless computing, and DynamoDB for scalable database solutions. Similarly, Google Cloud provides AI Platform for training and deploying models, BigQuery for large-scale data processing, and Cloud Storage for storing large datasets efficiently.

A key advantage of using cloud platforms is their ability to scale with your needs. For instance, cloud platforms offer elastic compute power, which allows you to scale up or down depending on demand. If your RAG system experiences spikes in traffic or requires more processing power to handle complex queries, cloud platforms can automatically allocate more resources to meet these demands.

This scalability is essential for ensuring that your system can handle fluctuating workloads without compromising performance.

Additionally, cloud platforms provide managed services for vector databases, like Pinecone, or storage systems like Deep Lake, which can significantly simplify the process of deploying your RAG system. Managed services take care of much of the underlying infrastructure, allowing you to focus on the development and performance optimization of your RAG system.

Creating a Scalable Deployment Pipeline

Once you've chosen your cloud platform, the next step is setting up a deployment pipeline. A deployment pipeline automates the process of moving code from the development environment to production. It helps ensure that your system is always up-to-date and that new versions are deployed smoothly.

For a RAG system, the deployment pipeline should include several stages:

Continuous Integration (CI): In this phase, developers commit their code to a central repository, and the system automatically tests and builds the code to ensure that it's ready for deployment.

Continuous Delivery (CD): Once the code passes testing, the deployment pipeline automatically pushes the code to a staging or production environment. This ensures that new features or fixes can be deployed quickly and reliably.

Monitoring and Alerts: The pipeline should also include monitoring tools to track the performance of the RAG system in production. If any issues arise, the system should automatically alert the development team for quick resolution.

By automating the deployment process, you can reduce human error, speed up the release cycle, and ensure that your RAG system is continuously improving.

Containerization and Microservices

Another best practice for deploying RAG systems is using containerization and microservices. Containerization involves packaging your RAG system, along with its dependencies, into isolated containers that can be deployed across different environments. Tools like Docker make it easy to containerize your RAG system, ensuring consistency between development, staging, and production environments.

Microservices architecture breaks down the RAG system into smaller, independent components that can be developed, deployed, and scaled separately.

This approach allows you to focus on optimizing specific parts of the system, such as the retrieval module, generation module, or database, without affecting the entire application. For instance, if the retrieval module needs to be optimized for speed, you can update and scale that component independently, without impacting the performance of the generative model.

By combining containerization with microservices, you can improve the scalability and manageability of your RAG system, making it easier to update and maintain in the long term.

System Monitoring: Ensuring Optimal Performance in a Real-World Setting

Once your RAG system is deployed, it's crucial to keep it performing optimally in the real world. System monitoring involves continuously tracking the performance, health, and usage of your RAG system to identify potential issues before they affect end users. Monitoring helps ensure that the system is always available, responsive, and delivering accurate results.

Key Metrics to Monitor

Several key metrics should be regularly monitored to ensure the smooth operation of your RAG system:

Response Time: Monitor how long it takes for the system to retrieve data and generate responses. Long response times may indicate issues with the retrieval pipeline, query optimization, or model performance.

Throughput: Track the number of requests your RAG system can handle per second. This metric is crucial for understanding whether the system can scale to meet demand during high-traffic periods.

Error Rates: Keep an eye on the number of failed requests or errors in the system. High error rates can indicate issues with the model, data retrieval process, or infrastructure, and require immediate attention.

Resource Utilization: Monitor how efficiently your RAG system uses resources such as CPU, memory, and storage. High resource utilization can indicate inefficiencies in the system or areas where scaling is required.

Using Monitoring Tools

Cloud platforms typically offer monitoring and logging tools that make it easy to track system performance. For example:

AWS CloudWatch allows you to monitor various metrics like response time, CPU usage, and error rates.

Google Cloud Monitoring provides insights into the performance of your deployed models and infrastructure, allowing you to set up alerts for abnormal behavior.

Prometheus and Grafana are popular open-source tools that can be used to monitor RAG systems in real time, with customizable dashboards to display key metrics and health indicators.

In addition to platform-specific tools, it's also helpful to set up logging to capture detailed information about system behavior. Logging allows you to track specific events, such as when a query is processed, which data sources were retrieved, and what the system output was. Detailed logs can help identify issues and debug the system quickly if something goes wrong.

Automated Alerts and Auto-Scaling

One of the most powerful features of cloud platforms is auto-scaling, which allows your RAG system to automatically adjust its resource allocation based on traffic and usage patterns.

For example, during periods of high demand, the system can automatically provision additional servers to handle the increased load. Conversely, during periods of low traffic, the system can scale down to save costs.

Setting up automated alerts is another important practice. Alerts can notify you when performance metrics exceed predefined thresholds, such as when response times become too slow, or when error rates rise unexpectedly. By receiving real-time alerts, you can quickly address issues before they impact the user experience.

Deploying a RAG system from development to production involves careful planning and the use of best practices to ensure that the system operates efficiently and at scale. By leveraging cloud platforms for scalable infrastructure, setting up continuous deployment pipelines, and implementing containerization and microservices, you can ensure that your RAG system is robust and adaptable.

Additionally, by monitoring key performance metrics, using real-time alerts, and implementing auto-scaling, you can keep your system performing optimally in a real-world setting. Effective deployment and monitoring ensure that your RAG system delivers high-quality, contextually relevant outputs while maintaining reliability and responsiveness.

Chapter 10: The Future of RAG: Trends and Innovations in AI-Driven Content Generation

---

The future of Retrieval-Augmented Generation (RAG) promises to revolutionize content creation and AI-driven applications in ways that were once unimaginable. As AI technology continues to evolve, RAG systems will become more advanced, efficient, and versatile, opening up new possibilities for industries and applications. This chapter explores the emerging trends in RAG, including the rise of cross-lingual RAG and other innovations, and how these developments will shape the future of content generation.

Emerging Trends: The Future of RAG, Cross-Lingual RAG, and AI Advancements

As AI continues to advance, the scope of RAG systems is expanding. One of the most exciting areas of development is the integration of multiple languages in RAG systems, also known as cross-lingual RAG. This innovation will significantly enhance the ability of RAG models to generate high-quality content across languages, enabling them to serve a global audience with ease.

Cross-Lingual RAG: Breaking Language Barriers

Cross-lingual RAG refers to the ability of RAG systems to handle and generate content in multiple languages by integrating data sources across linguistic boundaries. The goal is to create AI systems that can retrieve relevant data in one language and generate outputs in another, making content creation and data retrieval more accessible across different linguistic regions.

For example, imagine a RAG system that is used for global customer service. The system could retrieve information from customer queries written in multiple languages (English, Spanish, French, etc.) and generate responses in the customer's preferred language. This capability allows businesses to serve a broader, more diverse customer base while maintaining the same level of efficiency and accuracy.

One of the major challenges for cross-lingual RAG systems is ensuring that the retrieved data is contextually relevant and accurate, even when it spans multiple languages. Multilingual embeddings—vector representations that can capture meaning across languages—are at the forefront of this innovation. These embeddings allow the system to understand and process content in different languages while ensuring that the data retrieved remains semantically consistent across linguistic boundaries.

Moreover, translation models are evolving to improve the accuracy and fluency of

AI-generated content in different languages. As machine translation technology improves, RAG systems will increasingly be able to generate more natural-sounding, context-aware translations, enabling better user experiences across diverse languages and cultures.

In addition to cross-lingual retrieval, cross-modal retrieval—the ability to retrieve and generate content across different media types, such as text, images, and video—will be another key trend in RAG development. By combining text and visual data, for instance, RAG systems will be able to provide richer, more contextually aware outputs, enhancing the relevance and depth of the generated content.

The Role of Self-Supervised Learning in RAG's Future

Another emerging trend in RAG is the growing use of self-supervised learning. This technique allows models to learn from unlabeled data, making them more efficient and capable of understanding complex patterns in large datasets without requiring extensive human supervision. Self-supervised learning can be particularly useful for improving the retrieval process in RAG systems, as it helps models better understand the context and relationships between data points without needing explicit labels or training data.

As RAG systems move toward self-supervised learning, they will become more adaptable and capable of handling more diverse and dynamic data sources. This shift will also reduce the amount of manual effort required for data labeling and system training, further improving the efficiency of RAG models.

Real-Time and Adaptive RAG Systems

The future of RAG also involves the development of real-time and adaptive RAG systems that can continuously learn from new data and adjust to changing user needs.

These systems will be able to retrieve data and generate content in real-time, providing faster, more accurate responses in dynamic environments such as financial markets, emergency response, or live customer support.

The ability for RAG systems to adapt to new data on the fly is crucial for applications where the environment or dataset is constantly changing. For instance, a real-time stock market prediction system powered by RAG could retrieve up-to-date financial data and generate predictions based on the most current trends and news, offering more timely and actionable insights to users.

AI in Content Creation: Transforming the Way Content is Generated

RAG has already begun to transform content creation, and this trend is set to accelerate in the coming years. By combining data retrieval with natural language generation, RAG systems can produce highly relevant, contextually rich content across a wide variety of applications. As RAG technology advances, it will continue to shape how content is generated, distributed, and consumed.

Automated Content Generation Across Industries

One of the most notable areas where RAG is transforming content creation is in automated content generation. With RAG systems, businesses can create high-quality content quickly and efficiently, reducing the time and resources needed for content production. This is particularly beneficial for industries like marketing, advertising, and media, where the demand for fresh, engaging content is constant.

For instance, a digital marketing agency could use a RAG system to generate ad copy, blog posts, and social media content by retrieving relevant data from brand guidelines, previous campaigns, and customer feedback.

The system would then generate personalized content tailored to the target audience, improving engagement and conversion rates while reducing the manual effort required for content creation.

Similarly, in journalism, RAG systems are already being used to generate news articles and summaries based on data retrieved from multiple sources. These systems can automatically pull information from news websites, social media, and official reports to generate up-to-the-minute stories, enabling media outlets to keep up with the fast-paced demands of modern journalism.

Content Personalization and Dynamic Content Creation

As RAG systems evolve, they will be able to take personalization to new levels. By retrieving and processing data from multiple sources—such as user behavior, preferences, and demographic information—RAG systems can create highly personalized content that speaks directly to an individual's interests and needs.

For example, an e-commerce platform could use a RAG system to generate personalized product recommendations for each user. By retrieving data on user preferences, past purchases, and product reviews, the system can generate dynamic content that not only presents the most relevant products but also provides tailored descriptions, reviews, and comparisons based on the individual's profile.

This level of personalization is already having a profound impact on the way content is consumed online. Users are increasingly expecting content that is specifically tailored to their needs, and RAG systems are poised to deliver that in a highly efficient and scalable way.

Creative Content Generation: Enhancing Art and Literature

Beyond traditional content creation, RAG systems are also transforming creative industries like art, literature, and music. With advancements in multimodal RAG, AI systems can combine text, images, and even sound to create unique pieces of content.

In art and design, RAG systems can retrieve visual data—such as previous artworks or design trends—and generate new artistic creations that blend those influences with fresh ideas. These systems could help designers and artists explore new creative possibilities, producing novel works that are both inspired by the past and innovatively forward-thinking.

In literature, RAG systems are being used to generate stories, poems, and scripts based on a combination of textual input and retrieved data from literary sources. For example, an AI system could write a novel that draws on classic themes from literature while integrating modern references and contemporary issues.

The AI's ability to retrieve and generate content with a nuanced understanding of context will allow writers and creators to experiment with new forms of expression.

In the music industry, RAG technology is being used to generate new compositions by retrieving data from existing songs, patterns in musical genres, and audience preferences. This could lead to the creation of music that appeals to specific listener tastes or even pushes creative boundaries by combining elements from multiple genres.

The future of Retrieval-Augmented Generation (RAG) is brimming with exciting possibilities. As emerging trends like cross-lingual RAG, self-supervised learning, and real-time adaptive systems continue to evolve, RAG will become more powerful, versatile, and integral to AI-driven content creation across industries. Whether in customer support, healthcare, media, or creative fields, RAG systems will revolutionize the way content is generated, personalized, and consumed. With these advancements, RAG will not only improve the efficiency and quality of content generation but also make it more inclusive, adaptable, and contextually aware—ushering in a new era of AI-driven innovation.

Chapter 11: Case Studies: RAG in Action Across Industries

As Retrieval-Augmented Generation (RAG) systems continue to mature, their real-world applications are rapidly expanding across a variety of industries. From healthcare to finance, marketing, and customer service, RAG is proving to be a powerful tool for improving decision-making, personalizing experiences, and streamlining operations. In this chapter, we will explore several practical examples of RAG in action across these key industries, providing insight into how these systems are transforming the way businesses and organizations operate.

Healthcare: Improving Diagnostics and Treatment Plans

In the healthcare sector, RAG systems are revolutionizing the way medical professionals access and utilize information.

Traditionally, healthcare providers have relied on medical records, clinical guidelines, and personal expertise to make diagnoses and recommend treatments. However, RAG systems can take this process a step further by retrieving vast amounts of data from multiple sources—such as medical journals, clinical trials, and patient records—and using that data to generate more accurate, personalized, and up-to-date recommendations.

Example: Personalized Cancer Treatment Plans

A healthcare provider might use a RAG system to design personalized cancer treatment plans for patients. The system could retrieve information from various sources, such as the latest research on cancer therapies, patient histories, genetic data, and the most effective treatment options for specific cancer types. The generative model then processes this information to propose a customized treatment plan, considering the patient's unique medical history, genetic profile, and the most current clinical findings.

This approach helps doctors provide evidence-based recommendations more quickly and accurately, ultimately improving patient outcomes. By continuously retrieving the latest research, RAG systems ensure that doctors are always working with the most up-to-date information, even as the field of oncology evolves.

Example: Real-Time Diagnostic Assistance

Another example of RAG in healthcare is its use in diagnostic assistance. RAG systems can assist radiologists by retrieving and analyzing relevant data from a patient's medical records, imaging reports, and the latest research articles. For instance, a RAG model can analyze an X-ray image and retrieve related findings from a database of past cases, making the diagnosis process faster and more accurate. By augmenting the radiologist's knowledge with real-time data retrieval and generation, the system helps healthcare professionals make more informed decisions.

These capabilities are particularly useful for rare diseases or complex conditions, where finding relevant data quickly is critical for making accurate diagnoses.

Finance: Enhancing Market Insights and Decision-Making

In the finance industry, RAG systems are becoming invaluable tools for improving market predictions, risk assessments, and decision-making processes. By combining vast amounts of real-time market data, financial reports, and historical trends, RAG systems help analysts and financial professionals make better-informed, data-driven decisions.

Example: Stock Market Prediction and Analysis

In a stock market prediction application, a RAG system could retrieve real-time financial news, historical stock data, and company performance reports, and use that information to generate stock price predictions or investment insights. For instance, the system could pull in the latest market trends, government policies, and investor sentiment, then generate a prediction about how a specific stock might perform in the coming days.

By leveraging real-time and historical data, RAG systems can provide up-to-date market insights that traditional models might miss, giving investors a competitive edge in the market.

Example: Risk Management in Financial Institutions

RAG systems are also used in risk management to help financial institutions assess potential risks and develop mitigation strategies. For example, a bank's RAG system might retrieve data on a client's financial history, industry trends, and potential market risks. It would then generate a risk profile that could help the bank assess whether lending to a particular client is a safe decision.

This type of application helps financial professionals make better-informed decisions about risk exposure, potentially saving millions in bad loans or investments.

Marketing: Personalized Content Creation and Customer Engagement

Marketing is another industry where RAG is making significant strides. By combining data from multiple sources, RAG systems can help create highly personalized marketing content, deliver more accurate customer insights, and optimize campaigns in real time. This can lead to better engagement and conversion rates while ensuring that businesses are targeting the right audience with the right messages.

Example: Personalized Ad Campaigns

A digital marketing agency could use a RAG system to create personalized ad campaigns for clients. By retrieving customer data, including past purchase behavior, browsing history, and social media activity, the system can generate personalized ad copy and content that resonates with individual customers. For instance, a RAG model might retrieve information about a customer's previous interactions with a brand and generate targeted ads based on their interests and preferences.

The personalized content generated by the system can then be served to users through digital channels like social media, email campaigns, or website banners, resulting in higher engagement and conversion rates.

Example: Dynamic Content Creation for E-commerce

RAG systems can also be used to create dynamic content for e-commerce platforms. For instance, when a user visits an online store, the system can retrieve data about the user's past shopping behavior, preferences, and product reviews. Based on this data, the RAG system generates a personalized product recommendation list that is displayed to the user.

By continuously retrieving and generating content in real-time, RAG systems can ensure that the recommendations are always relevant, increasing the likelihood of a purchase and improving the overall shopping experience for customers.

Customer Service: Enhancing Support with AI-Driven Assistance

In customer service, RAG systems are helping businesses provide faster, more accurate support by retrieving relevant information and generating responses based on the customer's query. Whether it's answering frequently asked questions or assisting with more complex issues, RAG systems can improve the speed and quality of customer support, ultimately enhancing customer satisfaction.

Example: AI-Powered Chatbots

AI-powered chatbots are one of the most common applications of RAG in customer service. These chatbots can retrieve information from knowledge bases, previous support tickets, and product manuals to generate helpful and accurate responses to customer queries. For example, if a customer asks about the return policy for a product, the RAG system can retrieve the relevant section from the company's knowledge base and generate a response explaining the policy in detail.

These chatbots can handle thousands of customer interactions simultaneously, providing instant support and freeing up human agents to focus on more complex inquiries. The system learns over time, improving its ability to understand and respond to a wide range of customer requests.

Example: Personalized Customer Support

Another example is using RAG systems to provide personalized customer support. By retrieving data on previous customer interactions, purchase history, and service records, the system can generate highly personalized responses tailored to the customer's needs. For instance, if a customer reaches out with a complaint about a defective product, the RAG system can retrieve relevant order details and generate an empathetic, solution-oriented response that is tailored to the customer's past interactions with the company.

By ensuring that each customer receives a personalized experience, RAG systems enhance customer loyalty and satisfaction.

RAG systems are transforming industries across the board by enhancing decision-making, improving customer interactions, and driving efficiency. In healthcare, RAG is improving diagnostic accuracy and treatment planning. In finance, it provides real-time market insights and risk management. In marketing, RAG enables personalized content creation and targeted ad campaigns. Finally, in customer service, RAG-powered chatbots and personalized support are improving the customer experience.

The practical applications of RAG in these industries illustrate the system's versatility and potential to impact virtually every sector.

As RAG technology continues to evolve, we can expect even more innovative applications to emerge, creating new opportunities and efficiencies across industries. This chapter highlights the importance of RAG in transforming AI-driven systems and their capacity to offer practical, real-world solutions to complex problems.

Conclusion

As we conclude this exploration of **Retrieval-Augmented Generation (RAG)**, it's clear that this technology holds immense potential to reshape the landscape of AI-driven systems across a variety of industries. From improving diagnostic accuracy in **healthcare** to enabling real-time market insights in **finance**, creating personalized content in **marketing**, and enhancing customer support through AI-powered solutions, RAG systems are already proving to be transformative.

By combining the **retrieval** of relevant data with **generation** capabilities, RAG systems offer a dynamic approach to problem-solving, enabling machines to generate contextually relevant and accurate outputs. Whether it's retrieving up-to-date medical research to inform a diagnosis or generating personalized product recommendations for an online shopper, RAG is at the forefront of enabling more intelligent, adaptable, and efficient AI solutions.

As the technology continues to evolve, **emerging trends** such as **cross-lingual RAG** and **real-time adaptive systems** will further enhance the versatility and impact of these systems. The ability to seamlessly integrate multiple languages, media types, and data sources will break down barriers and make AI systems more accessible and valuable on a global scale. Moreover, advancements in **self-supervised learning** will allow RAG models to continuously improve, learning from **unlabeled data** to refine and optimize their responses over time.

However, as RAG systems become more advanced and pervasive, the importance of **ethical considerations** cannot be overstated. Ensuring fairness, transparency, and accountability in the design, development, and deployment of these systems is crucial to prevent biases and ensure that AI benefits all users equitably. By integrating strong ethical principles and bias mitigation techniques into the RAG framework, developers can build systems that are not only powerful but also trustworthy and responsible.

Looking ahead, the future of RAG promises even greater innovations. With **personalized content generation**, **real-time decision-making**, and the ability to handle multimodal data, RAG systems will continue to transform industries, making AI more relevant, responsive, and impactful. As these technologies mature, they will play an even larger role in shaping how we interact with information, how businesses engage with customers, and how critical decisions are made across the globe.

Ultimately, the success of **RAG technology** will be determined by how effectively it is integrated into real-world applications.

The path forward requires a balanced approach—leveraging RAG's capabilities to enhance decision-making, improve efficiency, and deliver better experiences, while carefully managing its ethical, social, and economic implications.

In conclusion, **RAG systems** are not just a passing trend—they are a pivotal part of the future of AI, offering a powerful tool for enhancing a variety of tasks, from healthcare to marketing. As the technology continues to evolve and improve, it will undoubtedly have a profound impact on industries and applications that rely on data-driven insights, ensuring that RAG remains a cornerstone of intelligent, AI-powered systems.